REAL CONVERSATION:
Eating Disorders

REAL CONVERSATION:
Eating Disorders

Biblical Truths to Help You Recover

Megan Johnson

RESOURCE *Publications* · Eugene, Oregon

REAL CONVERSATION: EATING DISORDERS
Biblical Truths to Help You Recover

Resource Publications
An Imprint of Wipf and Stock Publishers
199 W. 8th Ave., Suite 3
Eugene, OR 97401

www.wipfandstock.com

PAPERBACK ISBN: 978-1-6667-3642-7
HARDCOVER ISBN: 978-1-6667-9467-0
EBOOK ISBN: 978-1-6667-9468-7

To those who believe eating disorder recovery is possible
and to those who wish they could believe.

Contents

Introduction

Will you be my coffee date?

I once had a professor say that I ask a ton of questions. Her comment was, in fact, very true. I indeed asked her tons of questions, and I still ask tons of questions to this day. What grinds my gears though is when someone offers superficial answers to my questions. I am hungry for real answers; after all, I am hungry for authenticity. I am guessing you are too.

In addition to asking deep questions, I enjoy coffee dates. Fortunately for you and me, those go together quite well. I would like to say that there is something unique about that steamy or icy cup of roasted coffee beans, but there is not. It is on a coffee date, though, that you get to dive deep with someone. So, for the foreseeable future, you and I will be on a series of coffee dates. Each coffee date will answer a question that I have asked throughout my eating disorder recovery.

I am a Bible-believing, gospel-sharing, Christ-follower who likes having real conversations about tough topics. Therefore, this book is for women searching for biblical truths about a tough topic: eating disorders. If you desire a feel-good emotional storybook, you will not find that here.

From my experience, the women who will take the time to go on these truth-seeking coffee dates want help. You do not need any convincing that there is a problem. You desperately want to recover. Maybe you have hit rock-bottom or perhaps you are on the verge of hitting rock-bottom. Maybe you have mustered up the courage to say enough is enough. But you are addicted and trapped. You are entirely engulfed in an eating disorder, feeling weak and helpless. You are looking for a lifeline. Now what? I am here to tell you how I found a way out. I am sure you are antsy to get moving through this book, and I am excited to walk alongside you!

Likely, these women are not my only audience. If you are a loved one of someone struggling with an eating disorder, here is what I recommend. I invite you to read this book through your lens as if you and I are on these coffee dates. I have found that a loved one's actions speak much louder than words when recovering from an eating disorder. Not saying you do, but perhaps you have some recovery in your life that needs to take place before you can help someone else. After reading, I invite you to join me at the back of the book. There we will have a conversation about your role in your loved one's recovery process.

I am not a licensed counselor or psychologist, so I am not speaking to you from a clinical perspective. Instead, I am talking to you woman-to-woman, as if we are on a coffee date. Therefore, I am already invested in you. I genuinely want to be with you every waking moment and make sure you don't binge and purge or starve yourself. I want to be available to talk about every temptation and struggle that you have. I want to guide you on your path toward recovery and make it easy. But I cannot. The following coffee dates, though, are what I can provide for you. This is what I would have wanted for my recovery process. I did the legwork for you so that you may focus on directing your energy toward recovery. This process builds on itself and involves little steps that you take one at a time. I highly encourage you to take your time to reflect and act on what you learn. I am here to be your trusted confidant, encourager, and challenger. Now, let's get started.

COFFEE DATE 1

Megan, what is your story?

The obsessive behaviors began at five o'clock in the morning in fifth grade. I would wake up to do my push-ups, sit-ups, and squats. Each morning I would have to beat my previous day's record. Then, junior high came around, and I gave up sweets for Lent. It lasted for much longer than forty days. I never put sugar-laden foods or anything deemed unhealthy in my mouth until my senior year of high school. I relished my identity amongst my friends as the health nut.

I meandered on over to college, a university I had been eyeing since eighth grade. My classes were stressful. To cope with the stress, I began having late-night binge food episodes. When my roommate left to party for the night, I would hole myself up in the dorm room, shoving endless amounts of food down my throat. By my second year at college, the weight gain was noticeable, and I did not like it. But, giving up the bingeing was unimaginable. My classes were stressful, and my professors were demanding, but I demanded even more from myself. I needed to be perfect. So, I added a new stress-relieving behavior to my routine, purging. It was the perfect storm and the best solution to my insatiable bingeing habits. The weight fell off quickly; I felt thin, and I loved it. Granted, I had a constant stomachache, my teeth hurt, and I felt like I could faint at any second. But at least I was thin. Thus, the episodes became more and more frequent, occurring about five times a day. I also started working as a group exercise instructor and personal trainer at the university's gym during this time.

During this season of rebellion, I caused my loving, Christ-following parents much heartache. I lied to them a lot and drove them to many sleepless nights. It has taken years to mend those relationships. My younger sister, Rachel, wrote the following poem during this time. This poem perfectly encapsulates the hurt that my selfishness caused my family.

> Have you ever had your heart hurt? Have you ever had it ache? In so much pain, but nothing has happened yet; the pain is yet to come. It hurts; it just hurts. It's a slow tear, something you even saw coming. Something you chose to ignore. And you feel like slow ripping of your heart as you long for it all to just go away. You know the pain is yet to come, and you can't describe it any other way but pain. Your heart just hurts. It yearns for rest. It craves peace. All you want is to be okay. All you want is to close your eyes and let the darkness encompass you. Not watch the pain, and maybe you won't feel it. Have you ever been stained in your tears? Why do you let this addiction poison your body? They say once you start, it's like breathing. You must do it; you have to do it. Don't you realize you're slowly killing yourself? How stupid can you be? I thought you were smart, someone to look up to. Don't you realize you're tearing apart hearts in a family? Slowly. Slowly pulling them one thread at a time, a laborious and tentative heartache that never heals. They say you are healing, but you're not. I want results, and I want you fixed. It makes me so angry sometimes. Sometimes I want to run up and punch you in the face. Other times I want to hug you and ask you why? Why? Why? You don't see my tears because I have to hide them from you. If you saw me break, you would become even more broken. Don't you understand what you are doing? Not just to yourself. So incredibly selfish, but no, you can't look past that. The tears are staining my pillow now. An endless flood. I see the changes in your body. Your gaunt

stomach, your decreasing legs. I see it, and it breaks me. It breaks me.[1]

I was bound for rock-bottom, and indeed I hit it hard. I had rented a car one morning and ditched class to binge and purge over and over in a grocery store parking lot. I sped on over to the gym later that afternoon to teach a cycle class. I just about fainted while teaching. I then went to the library to try and study. But my mind was so foggy, and my stomach was in so much pain. I knew this was a low point, and I had to do something to get better. So, I biked home, called my parents, packed up my things, and was in their car two hours later. The next day, I enrolled in an outpatient eating disorder program.

The program was what I needed. It was the respite my body craved. The counselors at the program provided me with practical tools for eating disorder recovery. They guided me in lessening the eating disorder behaviors and developing a healthy mindset around eating and exercise. Also, while in the program, my counselors challenged me to get out of my comfort zone. It started with little activities like going shopping for non-workout clothes or getting frozen yogurt by myself. But one activity completely changed my life. I had briefly expressed interest in dating, so my counselor prompted me to create a Christian Mingle profile as a homework assignment. Within a week, I was talking to my now-husband, Ben. A month later, I flew from California to North Dakota to meet him in person. Six months after, I moved to North Dakota. Being that I gave up sunny California for the frozen tundra, this was indeed true love! We were married about a year later. While in North Dakota, I started the local university's nursing program.

Nursing school was incredibly stressful, and I relapsed repeatedly. It was my default coping mechanism when life got hard. Only this time, lying to my husband was much more complicated than lying to my parents. Ben reached out to our church and local counselors to get me the help that I needed. I reluctantly agreed to meet with our pastor's wife, mainly because the church was

1. From an unpublished poem by the author's sister, Rachel Ahr, entitled "It Breaks Me Poem."

conveniently located across the street from our apartment. During our weekly meetings, she talked about Jesus and the Bible; it intrigued me to read the Bible more. When I did, I constantly felt convicted. My lifestyle was laden with lying to Ben, reckless spending on binge food, and the constant need to affirm my eating disorder behaviors.

However, during that last year of nursing school, so much changed. The time between binge and purge episodes started to become longer and longer; meanwhile, my alarm clock went off earlier and earlier as I spent time in God's Word. It was evident that God was patiently turning my heart towards him. The Spirit of God was becoming a voice I listened to instead of ignored. The nonsensical food rules, compulsive exercise, and body image obsession became things I talked about in the past tense, not present tense. So much change was happening, and God gave me the fresh start I needed by sending us to Texas.

There in Texas, I was introduced to verse-by-verse teaching through God's Word. It struck a hunger to learn more and change my life to reflect what I was learning. I found the more I consumed, the more I wanted to learn and grow. I've been a Christ-follower since second grade. But I never felt an intense desire to pursue Christ with my whole life until then.

God is faithful and trustworthy time and time again in his Word. I consider myself so grateful to see that play out in my life. He was faithful in bringing Ben into my life as my best friend, encourager, and supporter. God was faithful in mending familial relationships. He was faithful in guiding me toward recovery from the eating disorder and drawing me back to him, his prodigal daughter (Luke 15:11–32). Out of obedience to his faithfulness, I wrote this book.

REFLECTION:

1. Question: What part of my story resonates with you?

2. Question: How has your eating disorder affected those close to you?

3. Question: Have you hit rock-bottom, or do you feel that you are about to?

COFFEE DATE 2

What is the root issue?

I spent countless hours discussing with counselors why I had an eating disorder. They said my eating disorder behaviors stemmed from a quest for unobtainable perfection, a desperate need for control, and poor self-esteem. You likely can resonate with these. However, despite the countless hours of talking and addressing these root issues, I didn't heal. In fact, I constantly relapsed. I won't deny that it was beneficial to discuss these issues with a counselor. But it did feel like a critical piece to the puzzle was missing.

I am sorry for whatever circumstances brought you to this point of having an eating disorder. It might be your upbringing, the ever-changing cultural beauty standard, or any of the reasons I shared. We could spend a lot of time addressing why you got here; perhaps that would benefit you. If that's the case, I suggest you seek a counselor to work through this with you. I, unfortunately, cannot do that on this coffee date. But what I can do is share what is at the root of your eating disorder.

Please know what we will discuss here today, I share with you in love. It might be harsh, but it comes from a place of love. I love you enough to want to share this with you. I care enough about you to share what is at the root of your eating disorder. Only our pastor's wife, a brave soul, called me out for what really was going on. She didn't sugarcoat the truth. At the time, the truth stung, but looking back, I'm grateful for her boldness. Now, it's my turn to be bold with you.

WHAT IS AT THE ROOT OF ALL EATING DISORDERS?

Sin lies at the root of all eating disorders. "For they exchanged the truth of God for a lie, and worshiped and served the creature rather than the Creator, who is blessed forever. Amen" (Rom 1:25). John Piper's commentary on this verse is helpful, "Sin hates the truth of God, suppresses it, and exchanges it for what sin loves and worships. Sin loves to worship and serve the creature, not the Creator. That's the root of sinning."[1]

This is called idolatry, which is worshipping anything or anyone other than God. Typically, the word "idol" conjures images of man-made pagan deities that the Israelites of the Old Testament worshiped. This is true. However, we still have idolatry today. It's not as obvious, though, as bowing down to a man-made block of stone or wood. Instead, today we bow our hearts to ourselves and our desires, not God's. This is what Piper says is self-worship, another word for idolatry. Self-worship is anything that serves us, not God.

The eating disorder is a form of self-worship. Let's use my examples from above to explore why. My quest for unobtainable perfection, desperate need for control, and poor self-esteem were all interconnected. I, like many women, sought to obtain the cultural beauty standard, specifically the thin and fit body type. I believed that I would be perfect if I was able to look that way. Therefore, I used what I could control—eating and exercise—to obtain this standard. I based my self-esteem on my ability to achieve it. But no matter how thin or fit I looked, it was never good enough. I constantly compared my body to other women. There was always someone who appeared more thin and fit than me. This led to poor self-esteem. I believed that I wasn't perfect enough and needed to work harder. This would cause me to spiral and revert to what I knew best—controlling eating and exercise. My self-serving cycle continued year after year.

1. Piper, "Root of Sinning," lines 191–93.

It appears, at first glance, that the cultural beauty standard is to blame. After all, if I wasn't receiving messages about how my body should look, then I wouldn't have this problem! The cultural beauty standard, along with a host of other things, certainly contributed to this. But notice that I was the one who internalized the ideal and held myself to it. My eating disorder behaviors served the standard I had set for myself. When it's all said and done, I was serving myself, not God.

The fact is, we cannot be preoccupied with serving ourselves while simultaneously serving God. "No one can serve two masters" (Matt 6:24a). I experimented with anorexia, bulimia, orthorexia, binge-eating, and compulsive exercise; bulimia, though, was my drug of choice. I ignored the conviction of the Spirit within me and continually succumbed to the desires of my sinful flesh. I was in a state of rebellion and self-worship. I certainly was not ready to surrender my eating disorder to God yet. So, for many years, I chose bulimia. I idolized the thin and fit body type, and it felt like every binge and purge episode pushed me one step closer to it. Despite how thin and fit I looked, though, I was never satisfied. This is why choosing to serve ourselves is ultimately pointless and purposeless. It will never end in true satisfaction because we cannot truly satisfy ourselves; only God can.

One day during a binging and purging episode, God placed a picture of my future family in my mind. I was married, my husband was at work, and I was bathing our baby. In this picture, I saw myself purging into the nearby toilet in front of our baby. Afterward, I wiped my mouth and went right back to bath time as if it was just part of our routine. That image shook me to my core. I was single when the eating disorder started, but I knew I desired to be married and raise children one day. The reality that this eating disorder was not just a casual fling struck me hard. This was a committed relationship to a sinful addiction that would follow me later in life. I imagined how my eating disorder would not stop when I got married, became pregnant, or had children. I imagined how the stress of being a responsible adult would only make me run to the arms of the eating disorder for comfort. I did not want that for my future family. I wanted recovery, and I needed to get better.

THE BOTTOM LINE: WHAT IS THE ROOT ISSUE?

The eating disorder is a form of self-worship, the sin of idolatry because it serves us, not God.

REFLECTION:

1. Question: I shared some personal examples to show how my eating disorder was a form of self-worship. What are some examples that are specific to your circumstance?
2. Question: If you chose to hold onto the eating disorder, how would it impact your life in the future?

Coffee Date 3

Why is self-love not the solution?

Dr. Jeffrey Borenstein of the Brain and Behavior Research Foundation defines self-love, "Self-love is a state of appreciation for oneself that grows from actions that support our physical, psychological and spiritual growth. Self-love means having a high regard for your own well-being and happiness. Self-love means taking care of your own needs and not sacrificing your well-being to please others. Self-love means not settling for less than you deserve."[1]

I was told that my eating disorder was a symptom of a much deeper problem. The problem was that I didn't love myself or my body enough. The solution was self-love. This made sense! I knew this was my problem. If only I had learned how to love myself more, I wouldn't have poor self-esteem or a desperate need for perfection and control. If I cared about myself more and cared less about what people thought of me, I certainly would not be bingeing and purging. As a young, malleable woman in my early twenties, I believed that self-love was the solution to my problem. I internalized this message and vowed to prioritize loving myself and my body more.

My life slowed down significantly during my time in the program. I wasn't a full-time student anymore, and I lived with my parents. My only responsibility was to attend the program and get better. This opened much free time to take care of myself and try

---

1. Borenstein, "Self-love," lines 4–8.

new things. The first thing I did was take naps. I took so many naps! My body was exhausted from what I had put it through the years prior. Since I was being monitored heavily at the program and at home, I couldn't engage in the eating disorder behaviors. It gave my body the rest and recovery it desperately craved. My counselors encouraged me to fill this free time with self-love. I never used to paint my nails, shop for clothes, or go for a leisurely walk. It was fun to experiment!

Here's the rub, though. Self-love is wonderful and certainly played a role in my recovery. Yet, unfortunately for me, despite all the self-love and body-love I could muster, I eventually relapsed. This is because self-love is nice and appears to be the solution, but in the end, it will fail you.

Self-love appears to be the solution, even amongst Christian circles, because there are two partial biblical truths hidden here. First, the idea behind self-love is that we are not worthless. This is indeed biblical. We are each made in God's image, bringing immense value and worth (Gen 1:27). It is biblical to take care of oneself through healthy habits like eating well, being active, getting enough sleep, carrying out purposeful work, and nurturing relationships. This is called self-care! Our bodies house the Holy Spirit; thus, we are called to take care of these temples so we may use them to bring glory to God (1 Cor 6:19–20). In this respect, self-care is a good and biblical concept.

Second, self-love is anti-conformity. It criticizes the culture and those in our lives for incessantly sending us messages about who we should be. When we listen to these messages, then it takes us away from being true to ourselves. This reminds me of the Romans 12:2 verse, "Do not conform to the pattern of this world, but be transformed by the renewing of your mind. Then you will be able to test and approve what God's will is—his good, pleasing and perfect will." The main distinction is that we must be true to who Christ is, not true to ourselves. Being true to ourselves is to be true to our sinful nature. This leads me to my next point.

The concept of self-love has two facets that are conflated into one: self-care and self-prioritization. In moderation, self-care is biblical. But it often goes too far and is taken too seriously. In other words, self-care becomes an idol. When self-care is elevated on a pedestal, this leads to self-prioritization, which is unbiblical.

The enticing nature of self-prioritization is that it promises immediate gratification now. It appeals to our sinful nature in that it serves us. Self-prioritization gives us permission to prioritize our happiness over anyone else, especially God. Does this sound familiar? It should! When you boil it down, self-prioritization is just another form of self-worship.

Notice that I was told to replace my eating disorder behaviors with self-love ones. The reason why I relapsed is that I replaced one form of self-worship with another form of self-worship. This won't solve my sin problem! Instead, this false ideology only perpetuates the sinful cycle further. I certainly agree that self-love is a temporary fix. Self-care, not self-prioritization, certainly plays a role in your recovery. It replaces destructive eating disorder behaviors with healthier ones. Of course, you will see results by doing this! If you want to recover and stay recovered, self-care must play a background role, not the starring one. In the end, self-love fails long-term because it doesn't address the root issue, which is sin. So naturally, you must be asking, "If self-love isn't the solution, then what is"?

THE BOTTOM LINE: WHY IS SELF-LOVE NOT THE SOLUTION?

Self-love is not the solution to the eating disorder because it is another form of self-worship.

REFLECTION:

1. Question: Have you tried self-love as a solution to your eating disorder? If so, has it worked for you?

2. Question: How could you practice self-care but not self-prioritization?

3. Question: What do you think the real solution is?

COFFEE DATE 4

What's the real secret to recovery?

I want to let you in on a secret. Well, it's a secret that shouldn't be a secret. The good news of eternal life through Jesus Christ is the solution to our sin problem. This is called the gospel message and was the real secret to my recovery.

God completely transformed me. He transformed me from a woman trapped in her dead sinful condition into a woman alive in Christ. Although I became a believer early in my childhood, that did not mean I was devoid of sinful behaviors after that moment. I was heavily entrenched in the destructive sin of an eating disorder from my pre-teens to my early twenties. I clearly tried it all, from self-help books to an intensive recovery program and a lot of counseling in between. But God remained patient with me as I sought other sources of healing. He placed specific counselors, mentors, and resources in my life that guided me toward recovery, but they did not directly heal me. The eventual gift of recovery from the eating disorder came about through a greater understanding and experience with the gospel message. Even still, this realization did not come about by my willpower or actions. Instead, it is a testament to God's character to save the lost and sinners like me. God used the good news of Jesus Christ to heal me and continues to walk with me by his Holy Spirit as I experience this challenging adventure called life.

We are going to look at Ephesians chapter two, verses one through ten. Ephesians is a letter that the apostle Paul wrote to the church in Ephesus. In this passage, Paul plainly lays out the gospel message.

> And you were dead in your trespasses and sins, in which you formerly walked according to the course of this world, according to the prince of the power of the air, of the spirit that is now working in the sons of disobedience. Among them we too all formerly lived in the lusts of our flesh, indulging the desires of the flesh and of the mind, and were by nature children of wrath, even as the rest. But God, being rich in mercy, because of His great love with which He loved us, even when we were dead in our transgressions, made us alive together with Christ (by grace you have been saved), and raised us up with Him, and seated us with Him in the heavenly places in Christ Jesus, so that in the ages to come He might show the surpassing riches of His grace in kindness toward us in Christ Jesus. For by grace you have been saved through faith; and that not of yourselves, it is the gift of God; not as a result of works, so that no one may boast. For we are His workmanship, created in Christ Jesus for good works, which God prepared beforehand so that we would walk in them. (Eph 2:1–10)

Paul starts his gospel presentation with the reality of sin. Sin is rebellion against God; it is a depraved human condition which we inherited at our conception. This is because we are descendants of Adam and Eve who committed the first original sin of rebellion against God in the garden of Eden (Gen 3). When Adam and Eve disobeyed God's direct command by eating from the tree of knowledge of good and evil, it affected their descendants, the rest of mankind. This includes and still applies to us countless generations later.

Only the perfectly righteous, meaning those without sin, may enter into communion with God and have eternal life. But "for all have sinned and fall short of the glory of God" (Rom 3:23). Because of our sinful nature, we all incurred guilt before God that deserves punishment. We deserve punishment, to be put to death and condemned to live apart from God in hell (Rom 6:23).

But God loves us and is merciful, meaning he withholds the punishment we deserve as sinners (John 3:16). He exemplified his love and mercy by sending his only son, Jesus Christ, to die in our place. Jesus came into the world as a baby born to the virgin Mary. He was a real person taking on a human body like ours (John 1:14). Yet, Jesus was perfect and blameless, having no sin (1 Pet 2:22). So, he was 100 percent God and 100 percent human (Col 2:9). Because Jesus was sinless, he was the only one that could be the ultimate sacrifice to cover our sins. And that is precisely what he did.

Jesus laid down his life for believers by way of the Roman cross, putting to death our sins with his death. Then, three days after his death, he was resurrected by the power of God! Jesus's resurrection from the dead is why those who believe are made right before God (Romans 4:25). Jesus is God's redemptive plan, a plan to reconcile us to him. Though we deserved death, Jesus died for our sins. Though we deserved to be apart from God for eternity, Jesus covered our sins with his blood, thus making us sinless in God's sight. Therefore, it is by no works of our own did we make ourselves right before God; Jesus clearly fulfilled that role (Eph 2:8–9). So, Jesus truly is our Savior because his work on the cross accomplished what we could never accomplish in our lifetime. As such, our sins are forgiven, and we can experience eternity with God in heaven (Eph 2:5–7).

While God is loving and merciful, he is also graceful in his plan to redeem humanity. His grace is evident in that salvation is a free gift (Rom 5:15, 6:23; Eph 2:8). Simply through belief in Jesus Christ alone may we accept God's gift of grace (Rom 1:16). This is called faith. If you believe the gospel message of Jesus Christ in your heart, then simply express it with words. Romans 10:9–10 says, "that if you confess with your mouth Jesus as Lord, and believe in your heart that God raised Him from the dead, you will be saved; for with the heart a person believes, resulting in righteousness, and with the mouth, he confesses, resulting in salvation." If you need help finding the words, here is a way to verbalize them:

God, I acknowledge that my sin separates me from you, and I repent of it! I recognize that no works would ever make me in right standing before you. Thank you for your love and mercy by sending your son, Jesus Christ, to die in my place. I believe that Jesus Christ died on the cross for my sins and put to death my sinful nature with his death. I believe that Jesus was resurrected from the dead, and his resurrection is what makes me in right standing before you. I, therefore, profess Jesus Christ as my Lord and Savior. I accept your free gift of salvation and eternal life. As a believer, I know that I am born again. Thus, making me a new creation in Christ, alive and new. Because of this new life, I desire to live a life that is pleasing and glorifying to you!

When you believe in your heart and confess with your mouth, you are spiritually made new by the power of the Holy Spirit (Titus 3:5). This is also called "being born again" or "regeneration." The true living God operates in a trinity, meaning he is one being who exists in three persons: God the Father, God the Son, and God the Holy Spirit. The Holy Spirit's regenerative work makes you spiritually alive in contrast to your former death in sin. As a result of this regeneration, you become a child of God, adopted into his family by faith (Eph 1:5; John 1:12). The Holy Spirit is a gift that God gives every believer. He promises that he will never leave us nor forsake us. The Holy Spirit is how we experience daily communion with this all-knowing, always present, and all-powerful God (John 14:17). It is also how we live a life that is glorifying to him (John 14:26).

As I wrote this coffee date, I prayed that all who read it would have a softened heart and ears to hear the good news. The reality is that I cannot force you to be receptive to the gospel message. While I am hopeful, I cannot change your heart, and fortunately for me, that is not my responsibility. God changes hearts and does the work of bringing you to life from your dead condition. My responsibility, though, is to share it with you.

THE BOTTOM LINE: WHAT'S THE REAL SECRET TO RECOVERY?

The gospel is the solution to our sin problem (Eph 2:1–10). Through Jesus's finished work on the cross, he satisfied God's wrath against sin. He provided believers with victory over their sinful nature. Our hope for recovery from the eating disorder is predicated on the gospel message.

REFLECTION:

1. Question: The good news of Jesus Christ is the most important, life-changing message you will ever hear. Reflect on this. Do you believe that you are a sinner in need of a Savior?

2. Action: If you believe that Jesus Christ died in your place, express your faith out loud to God. Use the prayer in this coffee date as your guide.

3. Action: Tell someone how the gospel message transformed you!

Coffee Date 5

How should I view my body?

First and foremost, eating disorder recovery involves resting in the work that Christ did on our behalf. It involves consistently returning to the gospel message for our source of hope (Eph 2:1–10). The gospel gives us hope because we are new creations in Christ. We no longer identify with our sinful nature. Instead, our identities are found in him!

Though, as new creations, we still have this pull to return to our sinful nature (Rom 7:14–24). Thankfully, by God's grace, we are not expected to fight our sinful nature all on our own. God has provided believers with the gift of the Holy Spirit (Acts 1:4). The Holy Spirit guides us in daily sacrificing our will to follow God's will. This means he leads us in aligning our motives, thoughts, and actions with God's vision and direction for our lives. This is a process of becoming more Christ-like, which is glorifying to God. The fancy word we call it is sanctification. The rest of our coffee dates, in fact, revolve around this sanctification process, specifically regarding eating disorder recovery.

A key aspect I'll share about my sanctification process was reframing how I viewed my body. We know the world worships our physical bodies as idols. Physical attractiveness, agelessness, and sex appeal are highly coveted. Beyond that, our bodies are viewed as our own, to be used as we see fit. The secular slogan, "My body my choice," conveys this concept quite succinctly. But this is all counter to a biblical understanding of our physical bodies.

As a woman obsessed over the thin and fit body type, I needed to learn what God said about my body instead of what the world said. Knowing these truths laid a strong foundation for the later steps in my recovery. Let's explore what Scripture says about these earth suits.

WHAT WAS THE ORIGINAL PURPOSE OF THE BODY BEFORE SIN?

"Then God said, 'Let Us make man in Our image, according to Our likeness; and let them rule over the fish of the sea and over the birds of the sky and over the cattle and over all the earth, and over every creeping thing that creeps on the earth.' God created man in His own image, in the image of God He created him; male and female He created them" (Gen 1:26–27). Our bodies themselves were not originally designed to be sinful. Adam and Eve had perfect bodies; they were image-bearers of the most-high God. Their original purpose was to love God and take care of his creation. God was pleased with his creation, both the world and the human beings, as he saw all of it as good (Gen 1:31).

In chapter three of Genesis, we read the account of Adam and Eve being tempted by Satan posing as a serpent. They directly disobeyed God's command and ate of the tree of knowledge of good and evil (Gen 2:15–17). As a result, their eyes were opened to their nakedness, and they attempted to hide from God (Gen 3:7–8).

WHAT HAPPENED TO THE BODY AFTER SIN INFECTED THE WORLD?

God laid out the consequence of such action in Genesis 2:17b, "for in the day that you eat from it you will surely die." But it was clear that Adam and Eve did not physically die right there on the spot. Instead, they experienced spiritual death, separation from God (Gen 3:8, 24), and an eventual physical penalty for such death (Gen 3:19c). As descendants of Adam and Eve infected with sin, we are born into physically alive bodies but spiritually dead. As one confesses their faith in Jesus, they are born again, making them spiritually alive with Christ (Gal 2:20; Rom 8:11). Eventually, though, everyone, whether believer or non-believer, will experience a physical death of the body.

WHAT HAPPENS TO OUR BODIES WHEN WE DIE?

The answer to such a question is entirely dependent on whether one is a believer or a non-believer. The non-believer, who remains spiritually dead, ironically, is unaware of their spiritual deadness. These non-believers know that physical death is inevitable and inescapable, yet, they remain ignorant about life after this one. They are unaware of their need for a Savior. Frankly, non-believers, upon physical death, will stand before God still infected with sin because they are not covered with Jesus's work on the cross. Therefore, their sin will sentence them to an eternity apart from God, which is called hell, a very real place (Matt 25:41; 2 Thess 1:8–9).

The believer, though, does not need to fear physical death. Because of our faith in Jesus's work on the cross, we take credit for his sacrifice that cleansed our sins before God. Our belief in Jesus's death and resurrection is the only reason that we may stand perfect, holy, and blameless before God after our physical death. After death, believers go to a state of glory in which they receive new, perfect bodies uninfected by sin (1 Cor 15:42–43). The death of a believer's physical body is a good thing, a blessing because it eliminates our sinful, corrupt body.

WHY ARE YOU STILL HERE?

After a believer comes to saving faith, why doesn't God just swoop her up and take her to heaven? Why does God leave us here? First Corinthians 6:19–20 answers this, "Or do you not know that your body is a temple of the Holy Spirit who is in you, whom you have from God, and that you are not your own? For you have been bought with a price: therefore, glorify God with your body." Our bodies are essentially on loan to us from God. We are no longer our own because we have been bought with a price, the shedding of Jesus's blood on the cross. We house God's presence, the Holy Spirit, inside our bodies. Therefore, the purpose of our bodies is to bring glory to God. In other words, our life's goal is to seek to please him by becoming more Christ-like (2 Cor 5:9). One fundamental way we do this is by exemplifying godly obedience in our thoughts and actions.

SHOULD I LOVE MY BODY OR HATE MY BODY?

body neutrality, but how can we achieve this?

Le Petit Prince

ecause we love and honor God, we love and that which he makes in his image. These nade in God's image do not entirely reflect fected with sin. Therefore, we should hate d our bodies because it takes away from , we hope and long for our future, heavenly be infected by sin. Today, by God's grace, earers (Jas 3:9). So, here and now, we must as given us and use them for his glory.

THE BOTTOM LINE: HOW SHOULD I VIEW MY BODY?

The purpose of our bodies is to glorify God. We do this by honoring our bodies and using them to carry out his will through obedience.

REFLECTION:

1. Question: How will you view your body differently now having this biblical perspective?

COFFEE DATE 6

What is godly obedience?

We learned last time that sanctification is how God makes us more Christ-like. He uses his Holy Spirit to guide us in following his will instead of our own sinful nature. While sanctification is what God does, obedience is our role. We partner with the Spirit in this sanctification process by being obedient. So, what is godly obedience?

I call eating disorders the "good girl disorder." In other words, good girls gravitate toward eating disorders as a form of rebellion instead of promiscuity, drugs, or alcohol. So, likely, you know how to be obedient. You likely are a rule-follower, a perfectionist, and know how to avoid trouble. Godly obedience is different than rule following obedience, though. Rule following obedience is simply right actions. "Godly obedience is characterized by right actions plus right motives."[1] Today, we'll discuss right motives.

RIGHT MOTIVES

I wish I could tell you that I was a good girl in eating disorder recovery. I certainly was not. To be brutally honest with you, what drove me to the hands of God for eating disorder recovery was not the best motivation. I tried different sources for healing, but none worked for me. The self-love solution didn't work out. Counselors didn't heal me, and the program didn't heal me. These were helpful,

1. Wilkin, "Should I Make My Child Apologize?" lines 9–10.

for sure, but they didn't solve the problem. As a nominal Christian who knew the correct Bible answers, I looked Christian-like. Still, my heart was not postured toward loving and serving God with obedience. Because I had grown up a Christian, I knew what running to God for recovery would require of me. I knew he was going to ask a lot of me. Notably, he was going to ask that I surrender the eating disorder and my selfishness along with it.

Self-love, my counselors, and the program didn't require this of me! Therefore, I avoided him. Like I shared in my testimony, I hit rock bottom hard. The snip bit I shared was just one of many low points for me. It wasn't that I hit rock-bottom, then I bounced back, and everything figured itself out after that. I repeatedly relapsed because I was not going to the right source for healing. Eventually, I did turn to God. But, it was more of a last-ditch effort than a holy and righteous motivation to please him.

I do not necessarily encourage this posture, but I tell you this to be authentic with you. I know the powerful pull of the eating disorder. Giving you a bunch of Bible verses and telling you what you should do is not a great motivator.

Eventually, God motivated me to surrender the eating disorder to him and pursue his will instead of my own. God was patiently turning me toward him and leading me to this conclusion. So, again, God gets all the glory for my story. I did want to get better, and I did often pray that I would get better. But I didn't know what that meant or what it was going to take. I just knew how dark, depressed, and anxious I felt while engaging in the eating disorder. I often cried out for help, and he did the work in bringing me to a place of repentance and the right motivation.

Let's take a moment to reflect on your motivation for recovery. You're clearly going on these coffee dates with me, which shows that you are motivated to heal. Is your motivation like mine in that you've tried everything, and this is your last-ditch effort? Or, is your motivation nobler? Whether you are the former or latter woman, I know that our following few coffee dates will provide you with some helpful and practical guidance.

Ultimately, I hope that your story is much more streamlined than mine. Even still, I felt it was necessary to be honest with you. If you can just run to God first, it will save you so much time and heartache. To do this, I encourage you to pray because God does most of the work here. Ask for God's strength, comfort, and peace. Ask for him to help you surrender the eating disorder to him. Ask for the right motives! That's the power of God because he changes hearts. He will change your heart to want to be motivated to serve him. It's pretty powerful when it does happen because it happened to me. And I'm confident he will do it for you too!

THE BOTTOM LINE: WHAT IS GODLY OBEDIENCE?

Eating disorder recovery is part of the sanctification process— when we obediently yield to the Spirit instead of our sinful nature. Godly obedience is not just right actions, it also involves right motives. When we engage in godly obedience, our thoughts and actions transform, making eating disorder recovery possible.

REFLECTION:

1. Question: What is your motivation to recover?

2. Question: What would obedience to God in surrendering the eating disorder look like in your life?

3. Action: Pray that God will give you the motivation to surrender the eating disorder to him!

Coffee Date 7

How can I avoid the eating disorder behaviors?

RIGHT ACTIONS BEGIN WITH A RIGHT MIND

Recall from our last coffee date that godly obedience is characterized by right actions plus right motives. We just discussed right motives, now let's talk about right actions. Right actions start with a right mind.

Our minds play a very powerful role in how they influence our actions. In fact, the Bible has a lot to say about our minds. Romans 12:2 says, "And do not be conformed to this world, but be transformed by the renewing of your mind, so that you may prove what the will of God is, that which is good and acceptable and perfect." Transforming our minds to reflect God's will compels us to behave in ways that glorify him. It all starts with the mind!

One piece of information I learned in a counseling session particularly stuck with me. Our brain is made of numerous pathways; some are strong while others are weak. Every time I acted on a thought or emotion with an eating disorder behavior, I strengthened that particular pathway. Over time, that pathway became like second nature to me. For example, I found that stress led to a binging and purging episode. When I started feeling stressed by the demands of nursing school, I sought a release. For me, eating a gallon of ice cream in one sitting, then purging it into the toilet provided me with the release I needed. So, when the stress emotion began to build up in me, I found myself driving to the grocery store for my fix. Every time I did this, I strengthened that pathway in my brain.

WHAT CAN I DO TO AVOID THE EATING DISORDER BEHAVIORS?

The tricky part is the eating disorder has already significantly manifested itself in behavior form. It is easier to rid ourselves of sin by attacking it at the thought level before it manifests itself into actions. This doesn't mean it's impossible; it just means recovery will take time. I want you to prioritize one thing for now—creating ways to limit the end result, the eating disorder behaviors. Limiting the behaviors will not solve the eating disorder, but it does temporarily provide relief. This helps you to think more clearly and open some time and energy for recovery.

As I shared earlier, being in the program and living with my parents prevented me from engaging in eating disorder behaviors. But, once I moved to North Dakota, I was not monitored and had much more alone time. I needed to learn how to be alone with myself and not engage in the behaviors. The beginning of this process involved putting up physical barriers. For example, I would do homework in a coffee shop or in the student lounge. By being around people, I knew I couldn't engage in a binging and purging episode. It forced me to find other ways to deal with stress. I would never eat a gallon of ice cream in public. So instead, I would get up and walk around or watch a few funny videos to get my mind off the stress. Over time, thankfully, that pathway weakened. I found I could do schoolwork at home alone without binging and purging.

Another example was after mealtimes, specifically dinnertime. I was usually tired after a long day and did not have the energy to fight the eating disorder. This might sound silly, but I found that cough drops helped me get through the hour after dinner. It kept my mouth busy, and the medicinal taste squelched my appetite. Again, over time, I didn't need cough drops. But it helped me get through that first phase of recovery. This phase is doing whatever it takes to avoid engaging in the behaviors. The goal here is to begin weakening those brain pathways.

Once you feel like you have a handle on limiting the behaviors, I want you to focus on lifestyle change. Next, I'd love to share with you some practical tools I learned that will help transform how you eat and exercise for the rest of your life.

THE BOTTOM LINE: HOW CAN I AVOID THE EATING DISORDER BEHAVIORS?

Prioritize creating ways to limit the end result, the eating disorder behaviors. This involves putting up physical barriers to make it difficult to engage. Limiting the behaviors will not solve the eating disorder, but it does temporarily provide relief. This helps you to think more clearly and open some time and energy for recovery.

REFLECTION:

1. Question: For you, what are three thoughts or emotions that generally lead to eating disorder behaviors?

2. Question: What are physical barriers you could temporarily put into place to avoid engaging in those behaviors?

3. Action: Be proactive! Set yourself up for success by putting up physical barriers before the eating disorder thoughts or emotions arise.

COFFEE DATE 8

What about eating and exercise?

As we learned, our principal reason for living is to bring glory and honor to God. "Whether, then, you eat or drink or whatever you do, do all to the glory of God" (1 Cor 10:31). We also know that our bodies house the Holy Spirit (1 Cor 6:19–20). Thus, we are called to take care of these earth suits so we may use them to bring glory to God. But we must be careful to keep our focus on God instead of obsessing over our physical bodies. The apostle Paul puts our view of eating and exercise into a godly perspective, "for bodily discipline is only of little profit, but godliness is profitable for all things, since it holds promise for the present life and also for the life to come" (1 Tim 4:8).

In the grand scheme of eternity, bodily discipline is of little profit. Paul recognizes the value of physical training but subordinates it to the more excellent value of godliness. So, eating healthy and exercising are not our ultimate purpose in life. They are means by which we care for these bodies God gifted us so we may use them for God's purposes. Ultimately, we are to be good stewards of all that we have; this includes our bodies. This earth suit is God's, and since it is his, we should strive to take care of it (Ps 24:1).

But here is the dilemma. Scripture does not provide a specific eating plan or weekly exercise schedule, so what is a woman to do? A good jumping-off point is to answer this question: is this eating or exercise behavior bringing glory and honor to God? The only way we would know such an answer is by being immersed in

God's Word and using God's gift to us, his Spirit (Matt 4:4; John 14:16–31). We will discuss how to do this on later coffee dates.

Each one of us struggles with eating disorders differently. The Spirit's convictions in my recovery process may not necessarily apply to you and your current situation. With that said, I would still love to share with you a few practical tools I learned in recovery. These eating and exercise tools taught me how to listen and trust the body God gave me.

EATING ON A SCHEDULE

 Going on an eating schedule was the first thing I did at the eating disorder outpatient program. It was one of the most significant, tangible steps in my recovery. I love how simple it is. You eat every three hours. For me, it was: 6 am breakfast, 9 am snack, 12 pm lunch, 3 pm snack, 6 pm dinner, then 9 pm snack. But based on your current lifestyle and wake-up times, that may differ. Try to eat your first meal, breakfast, within the hour that you are awake. Then, plan out each meal from there.

Imagine that your body is a six-cylinder engine that wants to run on all six cylinders. However, when you are engulfed in an eating disorder, you train your body to only run on one or two cylinders. By eating every three hours, you build a trusting relationship between you and your body. You communicate that it will be fed on a consistent schedule. Once your body trusts that it will be provided for often, it starts using three, four, five, then six cylinders to metabolize the food you are eating. Therefore, you will not become fat if you eat every three hours. Once you establish that trusting relationship with your body, then it will burn through your food faster than it did on one or two cylinders.

Additionally, sticking to a schedule clears the foggy brain that many women with eating disorders experience. It is tough to focus on recovery when your brain feels foggy. Your brain is a muscle. Just like your arms and legs, your brain requires energy like carbohydrates, protein, and fat to function. So, an eating schedule means a trusting relationship with your body and a clear mind. Both are significant stepping stones toward recovery!

INTUITIVE EATING

Walking hand-in-hand with an eating schedule is intuitive eating. Intuitive eating is listening to your body. Your body tells you when it is hungry and when it is full. It also tells you what types of foods and nutrients it needs. We were all born with this ability. Intuitive eating is not a superpower. Unfortunately, over time through various external factors, we stop listening to internal cues and instead focus on external rules. So, hold onto the hope that your body is designed to communicate with you. To get back to intuitive eating, you just need to erase years, even decades, of food rules. Learning to listen to your body and provide it with what it needs takes time and practice. It is very attainable and is a freeing way to eat.

First and foremost, continue to stick to your eating schedule. Then your next goal is to learn your hunger and fullness scale. For example, when you sit down for your lunch meal, rank your hunger on a scale of zero to ten. Then afterward, rate your fullness level on that same scale.

Zero means you are beyond hungry; ten means you are uncomfortably full. The goal before a meal is not to be starving, 0–1; instead, aim for the 2–4 range. After a meal, the goal is not to be overly full, 9–10; instead, aim for the 6–8 range. Write your numbers down.

Additionally, jot down physiological factors that accompany your hunger and fullness. Hunger is not necessarily a feeling concentrated in your stomach. Instead, hunger is an indication that your body is lacking the nutrition it needs to appropriately function. Notice if your brain feels foggy and if you are having difficulty thinking clearly. Do you feel dizzy or weak? Or, like me, are you plain cranky?

Similarly, feeling full is not necessarily feeling bloated and uncomfortable. Feeling full means you have satisfied your energy requirements for the next few hours. So, after eating, notice if you feel more energized and can think clearly. Or, if you overate, see if you feel sluggish and slow.

Next, choose satisfying food combinations by including carbohydrates, protein, and fat. Carbohydrates are the quickest form of energy. They provide your body with its immediate source of energy in that first hour. Meanwhile, protein and fat provide staying power. This allows you to remain satisfied and content for the duration of those three hours between meals. This combination allows you to approach your next meal with a clear mind instead of ravenous hunger.

Finally, adjust the content of your meals and snacks by paying attention to how hungry you feel going into a meal. For example, if you find that you are at a 0–1 before you eat lunch, then eat a more satisfying breakfast or mid-morning snack. If you were only to have a dry piece of toast for your breakfast, you are bound to be hungry in one hour, not three. But if you add a layer of peanut butter (protein and fat) to your meal, then your body has more sustenance to last for the next three-hour period. The goal is to constantly keep fuel in your tank. Your body does not want to run on empty. But it also does not want to be stuffed to the brim.

During this phase of my recovery, I struggled with bottomless hunger. I spent over a decade in the eating disorder, fluctuating between feast and famine. Therefore, I trained my body to suppress my hunger and fullness cues. As a result, my body did not trust me. Therefore, when I started recovery and tried to eat, my body went into survival mode. My brain was telling my body to eat as much as possible in one sitting. This is because my brain did not know when it was going to get its next meal. So, I felt like I could not trust myself anytime I was around food since I did not know when to stop. Accompanying this constant desire to eat, I would also become very anxious if I did not have food nearby in case I was hungry. Not only that, when I felt the slightest twinge of hunger, I thought that I needed food that instant. If you are in this boat, I completely understand where you are, as this is very common for women in recovery.

The hopeful news is that it normalizes. Eventually, that feeling of bottomless hunger or the constant need to eat does subside. Granted, it takes time, but as we know by now, recovery indeed is a process. When your body learns to trust that you will feed it every few hours and give it the nutrients it needs—carbohydrates, protein, and fat—it finds a nice balance. Your body will not tell your brain to eat as much in one sitting because it knows it will receive needed energy in a few hours.

NO MORE RULES!

We often hear the term "fear food" amongst women struggling with eating disorders. The irony is that food does not elicit fear. How can it? It is an inanimate object! Not only that, but we often attach morality to food by using the terms—good foods and bad foods. This mindset is embedded in our culture's view on food; it is, in fact, tough to avoid. It is inevitable whether you are on social media, in line at the grocery store, or chatting with a friend. Fad diets are one of the biggest culprits of this. Fad diets get me fired up because a fad diet is just another rule book. It places a set of restrictions on foods, food groups, and eating behaviors while simultaneously draining your bank account. The reason fad diets are so popular is that they claim to do the hard work for you. They give you a set of external rules to follow, that way, you don't have to listen to your own body. I once was one of those women enamored and distracted with the latest fad diet craze. I know how tempting they can be! While this intuitive eating route takes a lot of hard work upfront, it is a maintainable lifestyle, unlike fad diets. It is a lifestyle that allows you to eat whatever your body needs when it needs it.

Biologically speaking, food is just different combinations of carbohydrates, protein, and fat molecules. When you eat a fear food or bad food, your body does not press the code red button and say, "this must go to her hips"! Instead, your body sees the molecules and allocates them to suit your energy needs. Carbohydrates are the preferred energy source for your body, proteins help rebuild your body's tissues and cells, and fats aid with brain function and hormone balance. All these molecules allow us to think clearly and carry out the tasks we need to complete daily. The mechanism of action is much more complex than that, but the point is that a specific food item is not a fear food, good food, or bad food. It is just food.

At this point, I guess that you probably have been eating a lot of your safe foods as you try out these eating principles. These foods you will allow yourself to eat because they fall into your trusty set of eating rules and guidelines. But, in theory, if there are no fear foods, good foods, or bad foods, then no food is off-limits, right? So, I encourage you to slowly start incorporating foods that were once off-limits to you.

I did what I am encouraging you to do! I started incorporating a candy a day into my eating schedule. On my way home from school in the afternoons, I would stop by the grocery store and pick up one candy item. I allowed myself to eat all of it because it was in the place of my afternoon snack. I would go home and sit down in quiet and enjoy my candy. As I ate it, I asked myself if it was something I liked. Did I like the taste? The texture? How did it make me feel afterward? It was a fun experiment. I would sometimes try a different candy each day, or I would get the same one from yesterday if I liked it that much. At first, I gobbled my candy down each day fast. After all, I had deprived myself of candy for years in junior high and high school. Then in college, I only associated candy with a binging and purging episode. So, I had never actually eaten a whole candy bar and kept it in my body for at least a decade.

This process took place over a few months, and I learned some things. I got bored and found that I eventually did not want my afternoon candy. I found I would get quite energized after eating it, but I would be ravenously hungry for dinner. Or, if I overate the candy, I did not feel hungry when it came to dinnertime. Sometimes it would give me a headache or make me feel nauseous. So, if I wanted candy, I found I ended up only eating half, just because I knew how it made me feel the last time.

And then it clicked. This is what intuitive eating is! I was eating a food that I had either restricted or purged over the last decade, and it did not make me fat. Not only that, but it was not as remarkable as I had made it out to be. Did it taste good? Yes, some of them did. After that process, I learned what candies I enjoy and how much I enjoy before I no longer feel good. The foods that held so much power over my eating behaviors seemed less powerful when I just ate them. By giving myself the freedom to eat the food intuitively, it lost its emotional and moral value.

INTUITIVE EXERCISE

While in the eating disorder recovery program, I was put on slight exercise restriction. I had a very unhealthy relationship with exercise. I taught exercise classes for a part-time job during college, so I got paid to work out. It was an excellent deal, but not for a girl who was a compulsive exerciser. Knowing this, my counselors at the program did not permit me to go to the gym or teach classes. I was only allowed to go on leisurely walks. So, I would go on a walk when I got home from the program after dinner. However, I let it slip in a counseling session that I would make myself walk a little farther and a little faster each evening than I did the evening before. Not surprisingly, I was put on complete exercise restriction for a couple of months.

You would think that I would have been mad for not being allowed to exercise at all, but I was relieved! That voice in my head would not give me permission to rest or enjoy a leisurely walk. That voice told me that I would become fat if I did not exercise for one day. I liked being thin and fit. I enjoyed receiving praise for how healthy and fit I was, and that was my motivation. I held onto exercise so tightly that I could not voluntarily give it up. I also knew that if I did not have the time or capability to purge in a bathroom, I could purge at the gym on a treadmill.

Clearly, I made an idol of exercise. My exercise rules revealed that to me. My exercise rules were in place to help me achieve the thin and fit body type. I idolized that body type and welcomed praise when I reached it. But in the end, I was never satisfied.

I was not on exercise restriction forever. It probably was about two months before it clicked. I was in a counseling session, and I remember telling my counselor that I felt antsy, like I needed to move. I was tired of sitting and being inside all day. It was such a lovely day outside, and I felt cooped up. That was my aha moment! It clicked right then and there in that counseling session. My body wanted to move and be active. But over the years, I had squashed that natural intuition through an accumulation of exercise rules. I abused and manipulated exercise into giving me my desired outcome, an ideal body type. Ultimately, through my compulsive training, I had neglected to listen to my body. I was grateful for those couple of months of no exercise because I needed a physical and mental reset. My body required movement and activity after those couple of months. Because of the reset, I was able to build a strong foundation from there.

Part of listening to your body is eliminating the metaphorical noise, specifically external regulation. Intuitive exercising means that you do not need numbers to determine what your body is telling you. Just as you do not need numbers to tell you how much to eat or what to eat, you also do not need to rely on devices that track your steps, calories burned, etc. These are helpful tools that should play a supporting role, not a starring role. Since our goal is to build a strong foundation, let's eliminate these devices from your exercise time for now.

During those months following my exercise restriction, I was free to experiment. Most of my focus was on stress management and trying to get some type of movement daily. The biggest struggle for me was defining movement. Instead of always trying to one-up my previous time or type of exercise, I had to give up that notion. Instead, movement was anything that got me moving my body. That sometimes took the form of a leisurely walk, a stretch class, a hike, or a bike ride. Sometimes, I would be on my way to the gym and turn back around and call it a rest day.

This process was kind of like an interview. I evaluated the type of exercise to see if it was a good fit for me that day. Did I enjoy that kind of exercise, or did I feel like I just had to do it? One principle I used to keep myself in check was my one-hour timer. From the moment I started an activity to the moment I ended, it was exactly one hour. I could decide whichever way I wanted to utilize that time. Before, while compulsively exercising, I would have a workout in mind and would not let myself leave until I completed it all. This one-hour timer motivated me to work hard for an hour, utilize my time efficiently, and still give me the rest of the day to focus on other priorities.

Every moment of exercise is not supposed to be pleasant; after all, it is a discipline. But you can evaluate your overall enjoyment of that exercise. Also, consider your motivation behind it. Did you enjoy it because you felt thin afterward? That is not the motivation we are going for. Did you enjoy it because it felt like it satisfied your body's need to move? That is a good motivator. The possibilities of finding the right balance are truly endless.

Here are some questions to get you started in finding an exercise activity you might enjoy. Do you prefer to be alone, or do you like having company? Do you prefer someone guiding you, or do you want to exercise on your own? Do you like to be inside or outside? Do you prefer the gym setting or your home? Do you prefer mornings or evenings? What activity could you see yourself doing five, ten, twenty, perhaps thirty years down the line?

My goal at this point in my life is lifetime maintenance and balance. I am not a competitive athlete anymore, and I am not chasing a particular body type. I am just an average woman trying to find the right balance between activity and living my life. Even then, my enjoyment of exercise has taken on various forms throughout the past few years. Exercise for me today looks pretty different than it did a few months out of the recovery program. Right out of the program, I eased my way back into exercise. I experimented with different varieties to see what I enjoyed. I did not push myself too hard during that time. Honestly, it took a couple of years for my mind to have a genuinely healthy outlook on exercise.

Even today, I have to check in and ensure that I still maintain a healthy mindset and motivation.

In sum, intuitively eating satisfying meals on a schedule while incorporating exercise I enjoyed was monumental in my recovery. These practical tools directed me to listen to the body God gave me. In turn, I learned how to trust it and steward it, thus bringing glory and honor to God!

THE BOTTOM LINE: WHAT ABOUT EATING AND EXERCISE?

Intuitive eating and exercise are about listening to the body God gave us. Eating satisfying meals every three hours, conquering external food rules, and finding an activity you enjoy is a helpful place to start.

REFLECTION:

1. Action: Implement the three-hour eating schedule and practice intuitive eating with satisfying meals.

2. Action: Become aware of the external rules in your eating behaviors and slowly start to conquer them.

3. Action: Find a type of exercise that you enjoy and practice listening to your body.

COFFEE DATE 9

How do I control my thought life?

RIGHT ACTIONS BEGIN WITH A RIGHT MIND (CONTINUED)

Changing my thought life to reflect godly thoughts developed healthier, non-eating disorder brain pathways. This resulted in godly actions that fell in line with godly obedience instead of eating disorder behaviors that fell in line with my sinful nature. Working to control my thoughts started with listening to the Holy Spirit, then acting on it. Sounds simple, right?

I found this concept to be so challenging to play out practically. In my story, I mentioned that I met with our pastor's wife weekly for some time. I don't recall everything we discussed, but one thing stood out. Week after week, she would gently remind me to listen to the prompting of the Holy Spirit to guide my recovery. Week after week, I kept going back to her confused. I would ask, "How am I supposed to listen if I can't hear him? What am I listening for? I just don't get it"!

This is where my love of Bible study began. She taught me that studying God's Word is essential for listening to the Holy Spirit. The Spirit is God's gift to us; he helps us bring to remembrance all that we learn in God's Word. "But the Helper, the Holy Spirit whom the Father will send in My name, He will teach you all things, and remind you of all that I said to you" (John 14:26). Notice that this verse says, "remind you of all that I said to you." To be reminded of something, you must know it first.

The Holy Spirit uses thoughts to direct our behavior. But how are you to discern if a thought is an eating disorder thought or a godly one? There are two ways. First, God has placed a moral code on all our hearts. We intuitively know what's right and wrong, what's good and what's bad (Romans 1:18–21). Second, studying God's Word is how we evaluate if our thoughts align with his will or our sinful nature. As we go about our lives, the Holy Spirit reminds us of what we learn so we may act accordingly.

Let me share how this played out in my recovery. First, I was learning the biblical purpose of my body in Scripture—to bring glory to God. We already studied this together a few coffee dates ago! So, my mind knew what God said about my body. Therefore, when an eating disorder thought popped into my mind, I knew if it aligned with God's Word. For example, if I ate one of my forbidden foods, my mind would tell me to throw it up. Typically, I wouldn't even question it; I would just find a reason to go to the bathroom and purge. But, through studying Scripture, my mind was being transformed. The Holy Spirit would remind me at that moment that purging was not honoring my body. Sometimes I would listen to that conviction and avoid purging. Other times, I would recognize that conviction and purge anyway. I would always regret it, though.

Other examples include the Spirit gently convicting me to go straight home instead of going to the grocery store to buy binge food. He would speak common sense against my non-sensical food rules. He taught me to trust my body, knowing when I was hungry and when I was full. He equipped me in controlling my appetite instead of letting it control me (Gal 5:23). He would tell me when it was time to leave the gym or when it was time to take a rest day. Granted, I was not necessarily obedient as I frequently ignored those convictions. But God's Spirit was working in my spirit and renewing my mind. Partnering with the Spirit by obediently following his convictions led to changes in my behaviors and, ultimately, my eventual recovery.

Now, likely studying Scripture as the answer to transforming your thought life doesn't sound very satisfying. Perhaps you desire more personal and direct communication. That's called prayer, which we will discuss soon. Maybe Bible study sounds like a lot more work for you. I'll be honest, it is a lot more work. But it is worth the investment! Let me explain. Sanctification is a lifelong process while we live on earth. You aren't done with sanctification once you recover from the eating disorder. Now that I'm on the other side of eating disorder recovery, God slowly has revealed parts of my life that need to be more aligned with his will. He has shown me areas of selfishness, unforgiveness, and idols that have nothing to do with the eating disorder.

Beyond transforming our life to reflect Christ here and now, yielding to the Spirit sets you up with eternal rewards, not worldly ones. "For we must all appear before the judgment seat of Christ, so that each one may receive compensation for his deeds done through the body, in accordance with what he has done, whether good or bad" (2 Cor 5:10). I remind you of this not to fearmonger but to encourage a perspective shift. Let us be women focused on glorifying God here and now with our eyes focused on eternity (Matt 6:19–21)!

All that to say, to transform your thought life, you must be immersed in Scripture; there simply is no replacement or alternative. Studying God's Word does require time, energy, and effort, but it is worth the investment. I know you have the time, energy, and effort; you've managed to maintain an eating disorder after all! Now, it's a matter of rechanneling it for God's glory. Naturally, our next coffee date will explore practical ways to study the Bible.

THE BOTTOM LINE: HOW DO I CONTROL MY THOUGHT LIFE?

Right actions start with a right mind. Our thought life is potent in controlling our actions. We must listen to the Holy Spirit to transform our thought life. But listening to the Holy Spirit means we know what he is saying. We learn what he is saying by studying Scripture.

REFLECTION:

1. Question: In what ways do you notice that your thought life leads to eating disorder behaviors?

2. Question: How will you direct the time, energy, and effort you put into the eating disorder into Bible study instead?

Ash - reminded me
of you & how you
feel unsettled when
doing certain behaviors.
I think that's the Spirit!

Le Petit Prince

COFFEE DATE 10

How do I study the Bible?

My initial motivation for Bible study was more out of desperation. I was willing to try anything that would help me recover. However, my hunger to learn more grew as God was transforming my life. The Spirit's voice became louder and louder in my mind and heart; meanwhile, the eating disorder's voice started to fade. My life slowly started lining up with God's will because I was learning what his will was!

Hunger for God's Word works opposite to how physical hunger works. Typically, when we're physically hungry, we eat, and then we're not hungry anymore. But the more we consume God's Word, the more we want. I have seen this play out in my life numerous times. The more I'm immersed Scripture, I can't get enough. I keep wanting to learn and apply what I'm learning in my life. But, when I become lazy and undisciplined, I find I don't desire Bible study. My mind knows what it takes to get back on track. So, to be honest, I kind of drudge my way through that initial phase. However, once I get studying again, the momentum and hunger go into overdrive, and I find myself craving more.

As you've noticed by now, I like to emphasize where the rubber meets the road. Theoretical concepts are great fun to discuss. But if we don't know how they practically play out in our lives, they are useless. Regarding Bible study, I often found myself empty-handed and unequipped. I knew it was essential but was confused about where I should start or what to do. So, I muddled my way through it for years until I found some great resources. I love saving you time, so let me share with you helpful and practical ways to get you started.

WHY SHOULD WE CARE TO LEARN FROM A HISTORICAL BOOK?

I was one of those Christians that sporadically read the Bible. I would stick with it for a bit. Then, out of frustration and lack of immediate results, I would give up and turn to Christian books, sermons, and videos for my source of biblical wisdom. I would read books by Christian women for Christian women that would drag me on their emotional roller coaster ride. I would watch live church streams of celebrity pastors who packaged the Bible to be appealing and entertaining. I would even watch videos of Christian motivational speakers who gave me three steps in becoming my best self. I determined that I would figure it out when I got older, but for now, this would do. Then, out of guilt, during a significant life transition, and admittedly during eating disorder relapses, I would end up on my knees pleading to God for help. I believed God and his Word were just there when I needed him. The books I read, the sermons I listened to, and the videos I watched conditioned me to believe that the Bible was all about me.

If I were to keep making it all about us, then I am missing the mark. If I solely focus on the fact that God loves us, calls us, and has a plan for our lives, then I am not showing the whole picture. Yes, of course, those are biblical truths. However, the message of Scripture is not one of self-edification. In fact, the Bible is not about us. The Bible is a book about God. The gospel is incredibly offensive; the true gospel should sting. The more we read Scripture, the more we will see our own sin and shortcomings reflected. We should see just how much we need a Savior because of our sinful nature. That is why I do not skirt around the topic of sin. Sin is real, it separates us from God, and we must repent of our sin and believe the gospel. I care about you enough to share that with you.

This trend of deviating from the true message of Scripture is partly due to our modern culture's hunger for immediate gratification. We do not want to study or work hard to understand some historical book that seems to have no relevance for our modern lives. After all, we live in the twenty-first century, and Jesus came to earth about two thousand years ago. While Jesus's life and ministry are recorded in the New Testament, the Old Testament is even older than that. So, the Bible is, by our standards, really, really old! Why should we care to learn from a historical book?

The purpose of studying God's Word is to understand God's nature, character, and will. God is immutable, meaning that he is unable to change or be changed. God is the same in the past, present, and future. So that we may know him, God provided his Word for us believers. Therefore, if we approach studying God's Word to know this immutable God, logically, the Bible is relevant. Because God's nature and character are unchanging, the Bible is relevant to us today in the twenty-first century.

WHAT IS THE STORY OF THE BIBLE?

The Bible itself is pretty strange. It is very sophisticated ancient literature. It is not written in this time with our English vernacular and idioms. It was written by many different people, many years ago, across different time periods in other places. It is entirely normal to think that it is strange.

But, the Bible is also quite beautiful. It is a literary work of art that has transformed lives across time. As we learn more about the nature of God, we become enamored with this intricate and beautiful narrative that God orchestrated to bring us closer to him through Jesus. God did not just provide us with a compilation of sermons and a list of dos and don'ts. The Bible includes creation, kings, poetry, prophecies and fulfilled prophecies, the life of Jesus, letters to the early church, and a description of the end times. It includes people that succeeded and people that failed. God utilized forty different authors in different time periods with different literary styles to compile sixty-six books into one great work. Despite these differences, each book of the Bible contributes to the unified storyline—the depravity of the human condition and the hope of Jesus Christ to save humanity.

The Old Testament is a collection of books that describe the history of Israel—Jesus's heritage—long before Jesus was born. God wove together the Old Testament narrative to point the Israelites toward the coming of Jesus. We care about the Old Testament because it helps us understand the nature of God more fully. What we now call the Old Testament was the only Scripture available to the Israelites at that time. The law, historical accounts, and prophecies of the Old Testament all reveal humanity's need for a Savior and thus point to the hope of Jesus.

Jesus makes his earthly appearance in the New Testament. He is the ultimate culmination of every motif in Old Testament Scripture. The Gospels of the New Testament—Matthew, Mark, Luke, and John—describe what he did and said during his ministry on earth. These four books were written by some of Jesus's disciples, the group of twelve, that learned from Jesus and followed him during his ministry. So, each book is an account of Jesus's life from four different eyewitness perspectives. After the Gospels, the book of Acts details stories of Jesus's early followers and the early church. This is followed by letters describing Jesus as the culmination of God's plan and what it means to follow him. The last part of the New Testament describes end times in which we look forward to the hope of Jesus returning and ruling. Jesus will bring resolution, and the world will be recreated perfectly as God originally intended. Believers will live united with God as rulers over the new earth, and all believers will love one another.

As you begin reading the various books of the Bible, it can be easy to lose track of the main story. Everything in the Old and New Testaments point to the hope of Jesus. This story tells us what life is about and invites us to participate in this story. It is a story about dying to our sinful flesh and living by a greater power than ourselves. This is so that we may live self-sacrificially, glorifying God with our lives and genuinely loving people.

As we learn more about Jesus's work on the cross and how God wove this narrative together, his Word will change us. The divinely inspired words of Scripture that we have the liberty to access are literally life-changing. People, sinful people, who have read Scripture with the power of the Spirit, have experienced freedom and hope that no other historical book can produce. That is because God promises that his Word is living and active (Heb 4:12). Scripture is the active speech of God that is working upon us to bring us life. Reading and studying his Word rejuvenates and refreshes our spirit because it places us in communion with him, the giver of life. God is not boring at all, and neither is his Word. It really is just a matter of reading it and experiencing its beauty for yourself. I am excited to show you practical ways that helped me do just that.

HOW SHOULD I STUDY THE BIBLE?

Instead of bringing our immediate gratification mindset to the Bible, let us view studying God's Word like adding to a savings account instead of a checking account. Typically, with checking accounts, money goes in, and it quickly goes right back out. But with savings accounts, money goes in and stays there for a while until it is needed. Take that mindset to read the Bible. While you may not see immediate results from your daily reading, you are, in essence, contributing to your savings account of biblical wisdom, insight, and knowledge. This is because you are learning the truths of God's will. God's will is that we identify with Christ as a new creation (2 Cor 5:17). He does not want us to find our identity in anyone or anything else; this includes finding our identity in ourselves and the eating disorder. We learn what it means to be a new creation in Christ by studying the Bible to learn about God. When you study in this manner, you are fully prepared when the time comes to withdraw the biblical wisdom, insight, and knowledge you need. By viewing your study of the Bible in this light, you will begin a process of diminishing yourself and elevating God instead of the other way around.

Studying the Bible is not all that scary. You do not have to be a pastor or go to seminary to do it. You simply need the Spirit to guide you, eyes to read or ears to hear, and study tools you have learned while in school.

I recommend the New American Standard Bible (NASB) or the English Standard Version (ESV) as literal translations. The New International Version (NIV) is a good balance of thought-for-thought and word-for-word translation from the original Hebrew and Greek text. I use all three in my study because reading the same passages from different translations helps me comprehend them better. I recommend the Holy Bible App or the Blue Letter Bible App for multiple translation options if you prefer a digital Bible.

Once you pick your translation or translations, the key is to read the Bible consistently and systematically. Consistency is vital, so find a process that works best for you. Start small, like five minutes a day, five days a week, working your way through the Gospels. If you prefer an auditory method, I find listening to the Bible is very effective. One year, I enjoyed listening to the Daily Audio Bible. Brian Hardin of the Daily Audio Bible uploads a new reading daily, going through the entire Bible in a year. Every episode is a reading from the Old Testament, New Testament, Psalms, and Proverbs, in that order. The Daily Audio Bible is an app, or you can download the podcast.

Studying the Bible systematically is a solid gold standard. While in school, you would not just open your textbook to a random page and expect to learn much from it. Ideally, you would start from the front of the book or start from the beginning of the chapter. This is like studying the Bible. It is recommended to read a book in the Bible, like the book of Matthew, in order the way it was written. You would start at chapter one and work your way through chapter twenty-eight. This dramatically helps with comprehending and interpreting passages as you establish context—what happens before and after the passage.

The standard method taught amongst the evangelical community is to approach Scripture study in this order: comprehension, interpretation, and application. First, comprehension is determining what the biblical text is saying. You do this by establishing context, context, and more context. The immediate context of a specific passage involves reading the chapter before and after the passage you are studying. But before reading, the questions you should be asking and answering are the who, what, where, and when questions. For example: Who is the author? Who is the intended audience? What was the historical and cultural climate of that time? What is the purpose of the book? Where did the author write the book? Where was the intended audience located? And when did the author write the book? For answering the who, what, where, and when questions, I recommend reading the introductory paragraph in your Bible. I also highly recommend visiting The Bible Project. They create concise, informative videos that help establish this type of historical and cultural context.

Also, comprehension is about using study principles you have learned throughout your education. A great practice is trying to paraphrase paragraphs of the passages you are studying. Each paragraph of the biblical text is generally a complete thought. So, this practice encourages you to understand what the passages are saying because you have to put them into your own words. To do this, you will likely be looking up words in a dictionary to understand their meaning. You will also be studying groups of words looking for individual words or phrases that are repeated and emphasized, as well as comparisons and contrasts. As you move through the book, this practice will allow you to see how each complete thought flows from one to the other. By doing so consistently and systematically, you begin to accurately know the book's overarching themes while still understanding the details.

Second, interpretation is determining what the biblical text means. The interpretation piece flows from the comprehension information. The interpretation piece should lead you to answer this question, "What does this passage mean to the intended audience"? Context is key to interpretation. To understand what the biblical passage means, you have to understand what it says.

Knowing the context preceding and following the passage, and the historical and cultural context is crucial to interpreting correctly.

Third, application is determining what the biblical text teaches us about the nature of God. Let the comprehension and interpretation pieces guide you in learning more about God. To better understand the nature of God is the whole purpose of reading and studying God's Word. This is because learning about the nature of God through his inspired Word changes us. Learning about the nature of God teaches us how to live lives that are pleasing and glorifying to him. Application is not simply discovering the answer then moving on; it requires implementing it into our daily lives.

Do you see how skipping comprehension and interpretation can easily lead us to make the Bible a book about us instead of God? When we make the leap quickly, we will not extract the correct meaning and thus the application of the text. Instead, we will read with selfish eyes that seek to affirm lifestyle choices or worldly desires. We can read anything into the Bible if we take passages out of context. That is why context, context, and more context are so crucially important to accurate Bible study. Therefore, studying the Bible consistently and systematically puts our immediate self-gratification mindset on hold and teaches us to learn about the nature of God. This is how we slow our roll and stop the leap from reading a passage to applying it immediately to our lives.

To practice in-depth Scripture study using comprehension, interpretation, and application, I recommend starting with a smaller book of the Bible, like Ephesians. You may do this after you read the four Gospels or alongside it. Chapters one through three of Ephesians are about the gospel message. Meanwhile, chapters four through six show how the gospel message changes us as Christians, teaching us how to live individually and as a community of believers. At your own pace, break down each paragraph at a time, paraphrasing each complete thought into your own words. Take your time, do not rush, let this teach you about the nature of God so that you may be changed.

While your first priority is to read and study biblical texts on your own, I have some excellent additional resources that have aided in this process. For an elementary but impactful resource, I recommend a children's Bible! *The Jesus Storybook Bible* is the only one I recommend. It is theologically sound and beautifully written and illustrated. It goes through major stories of the Bible, showing how every story points to Jesus. I have learned so much from this children's Bible; I often get chills when I read this to my daughter at bedtime. As previously mentioned, before diving into any book of the Bible, I recommend viewing the correlating video at The Bible Project. They have clear, animated videos that provide a framework and essential context for each book of the Bible. A book that helped me practically apply principles of Bible study is Jen Wilkin's *Women of the Word*. She is passionate about biblical literacy and aiding women in studying the Bible for themselves in the manner it was intended to be learned. I recommend *How to Read the Bible for All It's Worth* by Gordon Fee and Douglas Stuart for a more textbook-type book. It breaks down the different biblical genres and teaches you how to study each type of genre the way it was intended.

Additionally, I recommend Pastor Stephen Armstrong, who started a ministry called Verse by Verse Ministry International. He taught through entire books of the Bible in a systematic, verse-by-verse fashion. He was our pastor while we lived in Texas, but tragically and quite suddenly, he passed away in 2021. All his teaching is available on the Verse by Verse ministry website and app. I like searching through the bible answers section of the website when I have specific questions. I also find myself at the Got Questions Ministries website when I am searching for biblical answers.

A couple of my friends taught me an excellent method that they use weekly. They study a passage on their own one day, then the next day, they listen to Pastor Stephen Armstrong's teaching on that passage. In this way, they practice Bible study skills independently but supplement them with quality, in-depth instruction. As a yearly idea, my dad has an excellent recommendation. One year, he reads the Bible in its entirety. Then the following year, he focuses on studying one book of the Bible. This has been an excellent practice for becoming familiar with common themes in the entire

Bible. But when in doubt, always go back to the Gospels to learn more about Jesus and the hope he provides for us as believers.

My goal for this coffee date was to make you excited to get started. Instead of feeling overwhelmed by the resources available, I hope this kickstarts your own Bible study with tools that have significantly helped me. It took me years to find these tools and explore them. So, I am giving you tried and trustworthy resources that fueled my hunger and desire to learn more.

THE BOTTOM LINE: HOW DO I STUDY THE BIBLE?

We study Scripture by learning the character and nature of God. We do this by comprehending, interpreting, and then applying the text to our lives. Context, context, and more context are crucial to this process of studying Scripture.

REFLECTION:

1. Action: Find a Bible in your preferred translation.

2. Action: Come up with a solid game plan to be consistent in reading and studying God's Word.

3. Action: Act on it by reading through the Gospels and studying Ephesians.

COFFEE DATE 11

How does prayer help me recover?

I learned, through studying his Word, that God was my father. This transformed my prayer life and contributed to my eating disorder recovery. Galatians 4:6 says, "Because you are sons, God has sent forth the Spirit of His Son into our hearts, crying, 'Abba, Father!'" In this verse, Abba is an Aramaic term, not a Hebrew one. The significance is that Aramaic is a conversational, common tongue, not the professional tongue of that day. This means that God is our father, our dad. He is not a distant father, he is not a supervisor, or a condescending authority figure. Instead, he is a good and loving father who desires a close, personal relationship with us, his children. God delights in a personal relationship with his children, that includes me and you!

During eating disorder recovery, I noticed a profound contrast between my relationship with the eating disorder and my growing relationship with God. My relationship with the eating disorder left me feeling isolated, anxious, and depressed. It most certainly was an abusive, one-sided relationship. But I found my relationship with the father brought me companionship, peace, and joy. I was listening to him speak to me through his Word and prayer was a way for me to speak back to him. It was, and still is, a life-giving, two-way relationship that led to my recovery.

Here's a question I often asked about prayer, "If one of God's attributes is that he is omniscient, meaning he knows everything, then what is the point of prayer?" My small group leader shared an analogy which helped me understand this. Imagine you compete at a track meet; your mom is there but your dad isn't. You end up winning the race! While you were celebrating with your team, your mom calls your dad and tells him that you won. So, when you get home your dad already knows the good news. But you still share it with him anyways! You have a relationship with your dad, and he would be so happy to hear it from you directly. This is analogous to how God works through prayer. He already knows what we're going to pray before we pray it, and yet, he still delights in hearing from us.

As with any relationship, the conversation starts out a little clunky but matures into something more honest and natural. The best way to speak to God through prayer is to practice!

Got Questions Ministries helps us understand how, "Prayer is much more than simply a way to ask God for things we need or want. Consider the model prayer that Jesus gives His disciples in Matthew 6:9–13. The first three petitions in that prayer are directed toward God (may His name be hallowed, may His kingdom come, may His will be done). The last three petitions are requests we make of God after we've taken care of the first three (give us our daily bread, forgive us our debts, lead us not into temptation). Another thing we can do to revive our prayer lives is to read the Psalms. Many of the Psalms are heartfelt cries to God for various things. In the Psalms we see adoration, contrition, thanksgiving and supplication modeled in a divinely inspired way."[1]

If you're unsure where to start, remember the example of the Lord's prayer which is to focus on God first, then yourself. I like to use ACTS as a template. A is for adoration, C is for contrition or confession, T is for thanksgiving, and S is for supplication. I honestly prefer a different order—ATCS—because adoration and thanksgiving are directed toward God, whereas confession and supplication are about us. Here's an example of a prayer during my eating disorder recovery. "Father, you are loving and good. Thank you for the beautiful weather today. I confess that I binged and purged earlier. I'm so sorry for not listening to the Holy Spirit

1. Got Questions, "Closer relationship with God?" lines 28–33.

when I decided to buy binge-food. Please help me! Please give me the strength to not engage in bulimia the rest of today. I need you and I love you. Amen."

Also, practice prayer as you read through the Gospels or study Ephesians. Pray his Word back to him. God delivered his Word to us and delights when his children meditate on it (Ps 1:2). Thank your father as you read, ask him questions, confess your sins, and ask for good and holy gifts as he reveals those to you through his Word. Even after you close your Bible, continue to communicate with your father throughout your day.

Recall from an earlier coffee date I shared, "If you can just run to God first, it will save you so much time and heartache. To do this, I encourage you to pray because God does most of the work here. Ask for God's strength, comfort, and peace. Ask for him to help you surrender the eating disorder to him. Ask for the right motives! That's the power of God because he changes hearts. He will change your heart to want to be motivated to serve him. It's pretty powerful when it does happen because it happened to me. And I'm confident he will do it for you too!"

Prayer will help you recover from the eating disorder because it changes you. Being in a committed relationship with the eating disorder will change you, for the worse. Being in a personal, ongoing relationship with a loving, good father will change you, for the better. This is because prayer softens and directs our hearts toward God, not ourselves. Prayer is a beautiful practice of our faith that honors our father and most certainly plays a major role in your recovery.

THE BOTTOM LINE: HOW DOES PRAYER HELP ME RECOVER?

Being in a personal, ongoing relationship with a loving, good father will change you, for the better. This is because prayer softens and directs our hearts toward God, not ourselves. We can pray using the ACTS (Adoration, Confession, Thanksgiving, and Supplication) model.

REFLECTION:

1. Question: God is a good and perfect father. How does this impact your prayer life through eating disorder recovery?

2. Action: Practice prayer!

COFFEE DATE 12

How does the church help me recover?

The beauty of this whole sanctification process is that you are not alone. Primarily, you are not alone because you have a relationship with a good and loving father. But God has given another gift to believers; it is called the church. Many from the outside looking in are under the false impression that the church is a bunch of perfect people that enjoy talking about how perfect they are. That could not be farther from the truth! The church is full of sinful people who recognize their desperate need for a Savior.

Jesus Christ is the head of the church (Eph 1:22–23). The church itself can be described as the universal church and the local church. The universal church encompasses all believers who have a personal relationship with Jesus Christ (1 Cor 12:13). Since we are in Christ, we are adopted into a new family, the body of believers (Eph 1:5). The local church is what it sounds like. It is a community of believers who live near each other and meet regularly.

What is the point of the local church if you have the internet? First, the local church is not the building itself; it is the people that congregate there (Rom 16:5). Second, God has gifted each believer with certain gifts that enable them to contribute to the body of believers (1 Cor 12:7). So, each member plays a role in supporting, encouraging, and strengthening the body so that the church can spread the good news of Jesus Christ. Of course, you may find encouragement and knowledge by watching or listening to a sermon online; however, you are missing out on two benefits.

You are missing out on the ability to discover your God-given gifts and use them to love others. You are also missing out on reaping the benefits of the gifts of others.

I am very introverted, as my natural inclination is to be by myself. I feel energized when I have many hours alone to read, study, listen, and write. This personality trait has lent itself well to making time for studying God's Word and meditating on it. That comes relatively easy for me. However, spending time with other people and serving them is pretty exhausting for me. Therefore, I do not jump at the opportunity to go to a small-group Bible study or church.

While my personality comes with its strengths and weaknesses, God uses both for his glory. The strength of my introversion is that I spend much time studying God's Word and use it as a framework to analyze the world around me. Instead of keeping this knowledge to myself, I share it with others, hence this book! However, a weakness of my introversion is that I prefer isolation over fellowship with other believers. But God has called all believers to meet together to love and encourage one another to do the good works God planned for us (Heb 10:24–25, Eph 2:10). God has used my husband, who is quite extroverted, to help me in my weakness. My husband is a fellow believer and thus my brother-in-Christ. He uses his gifts to encourage me to obey God's command to serve and assemble with other believers.

Additionally, I have been significantly impacted by two women within the church body. Clearly, our pastor's wife had a significant impact on my life. Her gifting in mentorship led me to seek Scripture. I have also been significantly impacted by Jen Wilkin and her mission to enhance Bible literacy among women. Both these women and their ministries have directed me toward Scripture which was instrumental to my recovery.

Suppose you would like some guidance in finding a church. In that case, I suggest that you look for a fellowship of Christ-centered believers who teach directly from the Word of God, and share the gospel with the local community. The teaching should guide you in Scripture and equip you to use your time here on earth to bring glory to God. An excellent resource for finding such a church is the website, 9Marks, under the church search menu. If you are a college student, a local church is highly recommended, but also look into your campus's church organizations. Often, these organizations host small groups by dorm or major, have weekly gatherings, built-in social activities, and attend the same church together.

Once you find this community, then get involved by devoting your time, talent, and treasure. There are many needs within the church body, and there are always opportunities to serve. You do this out of reverence and obedience to Christ. If you attend, volunteer, or donate to the church out of obligation, then just stop. Don't do that. Jesus did the hard work of dying on the cross. He desires you to genuinely have a heart for serving him. He does not want you helping or giving out of guilt. By doing so, you only serve a guilty conscience which does nothing to further the kingdom.

I begrudgingly followed Ben to church early in our marriage because I felt like I had to. Ben prayed that my heart would be transformed to want to serve God through the church community. It was not an overnight experience, but my heart did change. Over time, and this is no surprise, I found that I prefer behind-the-scenes service while Ben likes being around people. For example, at our last church, we served at the coffee bar. I worked behind the counter making coffee drinks. Meanwhile, Ben was at the front, taking orders and chatting with people in line. We love serving together, but we know that we have different God-given gifts.

God has also used the church to bring about my strongest and closest friendships with other women. They have been such a gift from God during different seasons of my life! These friendships are unique because we both know and acknowledge that we are sinful women. Yet, we desire to use our God-given gifts to encourage one another to fight our sinful flesh and walk the godly path. That is why conversations with these women can get deep very quickly, or they can be superficial. We can talk about sin we are struggling with or talk about our favorite coffee shops (Jas 5:16).

Women struggling with eating disorders often do so in secret and prefer isolation. Therefore, finding and getting involved in a local church is a method God uses to sanctify us, making us more like Jesus Christ, the head of our church. So, I highly encourage you to find a local community of believers, get involved, and make friendships with other women. If you feel comfortable, be honest with those women you trust about your eating disorder struggle. Expose the sin of the eating disorder and ask those women to pray for you and hold you accountable (Eph 5:11).

Having an accountability partner was simultaneously annoying and fruitful. It was annoying when I engaged in the eating disorder; it was fruitful when I needed the nudge to choose God's will, not my own. Indeed, I was cautious with whom I confided in about my daily struggle with bulimia. Our pastor's wife and her husband moved to another town, and God brought another mentor into my life quickly after that. I immediately felt safe with her and confided in her. She would have me over for coffee, check in with me when Ben was out of town, and send me encouragement when nursing school was particularly stressful. She became a big part of my life, and I became a big part of hers. Our husbands also happened to get along, and we still maintain our friendship to this day, even hundreds of miles apart!

THE BOTTOM LINE: HOW DOES THE CHURCH HELP ME RECOVER?

Fellowship with other believers is glorifying to God. It helps with accountability to sin and provides a safe place to learn, grow, and be sanctified.

REFLECTION:

1. Question: What are some strengths and weaknesses of the giftings God has given you?

2. Question: How will you use these giftings for the benefit of the church body?

3. Action: Find a local church community and get plugged into a small group! If you are already in a church community, pray for and seek a woman to mentor you.

COFFEE DATE 13

When am I recovered?

"When am I recovered"? is a question I often receive. It's a natural question to ask, of course. As you can imagine, I've asked this question myself countless times! Let's look at Scripture to find the answer.

Ephesians 4:22–24 says, "in reference to your former manner of life, you lay aside the old self, which is being corrupted in accordance with the lusts of deceit, and that you be renewed in the spirit of your mind, and put on the new self, which in the likeness of God has been created in righteousness and holiness of the truth." We, believers, are new creations when we confess Jesus Christ as our Lord and Savior (2 Cor 5:17). We are not a new creation once we eventually recover from the eating disorder. Eating disorder recovery is part of the sanctification process; it is not a salvation requirement. But, despite us being new creations, Paul constantly reminds believers to put off the old self and put on the new self (Rom 6:6, 13:14; Eph 4:22–24; Col 3:9–10). Why would that be?

There is still tension between the Spirit within us and our sinful nature (Rom 7:14–25). We struggle with the temptation of returning to our old practices of sinful idolatry. But temptation itself is not a sin. Jesus was tempted, and yet he was sinless (Heb 4:15). Instead, the temptation can lead us to sin. Since the Spirit of God takes up residence in our hearts, he supplies us with the power to overcome the pull of our sinful nature (2 Cor 10:3–5; 1 John 3:9). When we are tempted and fall into sin, God's Spirit convicts us and leads us to repentance (Rom 2:4). When we confess our sins to God, he forgives and cleanses us (1 John 1:9), not because we deserve it, but because of his loving nature.

I remind you of all these biblical truths because the temptation to revert to eating disorder behaviors will be powerful at times. Relapses may occur but remember that you are already a new creation. If you relapse, confess your sins to God through prayer, then move on. You might be tempted to run, hide, and isolate yourself from God when you relapse. I tell you from personal experience that it is not worth it! Through Jesus's finished work on the cross, he satisfied God's wrath against all sin, including relapses. He provided believers with victory over their sinful nature. We were once dead in our sins but now are alive together with Christ (Eph 2:5). "Therefore there is now no condemnation for those who are in Christ Jesus" (Rom 8:1)!

True healing and freedom from the eating disorder cannot be obtained through human effort alone. Healing from an eating disorder is not something you may conjure up on your own through more self-love. It does not involve gritting your teeth and doubling your efforts. Freedom is only found by being satisfied in the person and work of Christ. Therefore, constantly return to the message of the gospel, Ephesians 2:1–10, for your source of hope during recovery.

The answer to the big question remains. When are you officially recovered? Because sanctification is an ongoing process, there is no exact moment in which a woman is fully recovered. For me, I saw much progress when my obsessive bingeing and purging behaviors started to diminish. The time between episodes began to grow longer and longer. Today, I do not struggle with overt eating disorder behaviors; therefore, I consider myself recovered in that regard. However, I do still struggle with finding a balance between healthy eating and exercising regularly. Sometimes I toe the line between being too relaxed; more often than not, I am too rigid. Sometimes, I idolize the thin and fit body type and compare my body to women on social media. So, there are many ways that

God's Spirit continues to work in sanctifying me when it comes to my body.

While we live here on earth, we will always live in that tension between our dead sinful nature and God's life-giving Spirit within us. The Spirit directs us to lead a life that is pleasing and glorifying to God; this is sanctification! We are to learn from our mistakes and use them for his glory. This is why I wrote these coffee dates for you, and I hope you enjoyed them as much as I did.

THE BOTTOM LINE: WHEN AM I RECOVERED?

The temptation to revert to eating disorder behaviors will be powerful at times. Relapses may occur but remember that you are already a new creation. If you relapse, confess your sins to God through prayer, then move on. Freedom from the eating disorder is only found by being satisfied in the person and work of Christ. Therefore, constantly return to the message of the gospel (Eph 2:1–10) for your source of hope during recovery.

REFLECTION:

1. Question: What are practical ways that you could avoid the temptation of the eating disorder?

2. Action: Continue to implement actions that make it difficult to engage in eating disorder behaviors.

3. Action: Keep Ephesians 2:1–10 nearby so you can reach for it in the face of temptation.

4. Action: If you relapse, quickly confess your sin to God through prayer and move on.

Summary

We covered a lot during our time together! Since this is a resource, I want to provide you with a quick version of our coffee dates to consult in a pinch. Let's cover the main points we discussed.

MAIN POINTS:

1. What is the root issue? The eating disorder is a form of self-worship, the sin of idolatry because it serves us, not God.

2. Why is self-love not the solution? Self-love is not the solution to the eating disorder because it is another form of self-worship.

3. What's the real secret to recovery? The gospel is the solution to our sin problem (Eph 2:1–10). Through Jesus's finished work on the cross, he satisfied God's wrath against sin. He provided believers with victory over their sinful nature. Our hope for recovery from the eating disorder is predicated on the gospel message.

4. How should I view my body? The purpose of our bodies is to glorify God. We do this by honoring our bodies and using them to carry out his will through obedience.

5. What is godly obedience? Eating disorder recovery is part of the sanctification process—when we obediently yield to the Spirit instead of our sinful nature. Godly obedience is not just right actions, it also involves right motives. When we engage

in godly obedience, our thoughts and actions transform, making eating disorder recovery possible.

6. How can I avoid the eating disorder behaviors? Prioritize creating ways to limit the end result, the eating disorder behaviors. This involves putting up physical barriers to make it difficult to engage. Limiting the behaviors will not solve the eating disorder, but it does temporarily provide relief. This helps you to think more clearly and open some time and energy for recovery.

7. What about eating and exercise? Intuitive eating and exercise are about listening to the body God gave us. Eating satisfying meals every three hours, conquering external food rules, and finding an activity you enjoy is a helpful place to start.

8. How do I control my thought life? Right actions start with a right mind. Our thought life is potent in controlling our actions. We must listen to the Holy Spirit to transform our thought life. But listening to the Holy Spirit means we know what he is saying. We learn what he is saying by studying Scripture.

9. How do I study the Bible? We study Scripture by learning the character and nature of God. We do this by comprehending, interpreting, and then applying the text to our lives. Context, context, and more context are crucial to this process of studying Scripture.

10. How does prayer help me recover? Being in a personal, ongoing relationship with a loving, good father will change you, for the better. This is because prayer softens and directs our hearts toward God, not ourselves. We can pray using the ACTS (Adoration, Confession, Thanksgiving, and Supplication) model.

11. How does the church help me recover? Fellowship with other believers is glorifying to God. It helps with accountability to sin and provides a safe place to learn, grow, and be sanctified.

12. When am I recovered? The temptation to revert to eating disorder behaviors will be powerful at times. Relapses may occur but remember that you are already a new creation. If you relapse, confess your sins to God through prayer, then move on. Freedom from the eating disorder is only found by being satisfied in the person and work of Christ. Therefore, constantly return to the message of the gospel (Eph 2:1–10) for your source of hope during recovery.

CONVERSATION WITH LOVED ONES

Welcome loved ones! Thanks for joining me. If you are looking for the magic secret, it is not here. The best advice I can give you though is this: check yourself, connect her with a counselor or mentor, and surrender it to God.

CHECK YOURSELF

Before flipping to this section, I first invite you to read all the coffee dates through your lens. Perhaps you have some recovery that needs to occur first before shifting your attention to your loved one. If this is an area you struggle in, pray that God will change your heart and behaviors! This is all part of the sanctification process as Christ-followers. Ask the Holy Spirit to guide you in setting a genuine, godly example for your loved one.

You likely spend a lot of time with your loved one. She is watching and listening to you. She is listening to how you talk about food, exercise, and your body. And, she knows when you are being genuine. If you know the right words to say but act very differently, she will see the hypocrisy. For example, she notices that fad diet book sitting on your nightstand. If you spend countless hours at the gym, she notices that. Or, if you talk about how beautiful she is but she catches you comparing yourself to other women on social media, she sees that.

Ultimately, recognize that our bodies are temporary loans from God for us to use in sharing the gospel message. Keeping this eternal perspective with a biblical view of our bodies is crucial for setting a godly example for your loved one.

CONNECT HER WITH A COUNSELOR OR MENTOR

I asked Ben for his two cents. He said, "You cannot fix the eating disorder for them. And when they mess up, which they will, then be careful how you respond to the relapse. If you blame the person, it creates a divide, if you care for them and pray for them, it brings you together."

If you want your loved one to come to you when struggling or relapsing, be careful how you respond. It is so easy to say, "snap out of it, just eat, stop throwing up, or stop exercising." But she is trapped inside her mind, in a very different reality. If she feels comfortable, invite her to explain her reality out loud to you. Instead of inserting your logic and reason, be her trusted confidant by listening.

Now, if you cannot bear this role or if your loved one does not want you to take on this role, then help her find a trusted counselor or mentor. Sometimes children cannot hear it from their parents, or a wife cannot hear it from her husband. I was incredibly stubborn to Ben's support and encouragement. Your loved one might need someone else in her life telling her the same thing you would.

As you read this book, you will notice that I do not encourage women to go rummaging in their past to find someone or some circumstance to blame for their eating disorder. The reality is that your loved one has an eating disorder here and now. Pinpointing someone or a specific event is only going to displace blame and prolong her recovery process. Once she realizes that no one is starving her or forcing her to over-eat or purge, she must recognize that she is responsible for her actions.

But just because I am not encouraging her to blame someone does not mean others will do the same. Therefore, I recommend you find a counselor who uses cognitive behavioral therapy (CBT) over psychoanalysis. CBT aims to change her thought patterns to ultimately lessen her eating disorder behaviors. CBT does involve examining circumstances that lead to the eating disorder, but that is not the sole focus. On the other hand, psychoanalysis delves into her childhood to identify how her subconscious influences her eating disorder behaviors. This may be helpful for some women, but it will take much longer to see tangible results. Take this example. A newly diagnosed cancer patient goes to her doctor. The doctor starts her on a chemotherapy treatment plan to directly target the cancer cells. The doctor won't spend countless appointments pinpointing why she has cancer. The doctor may spend some time doing this, but the main focus is on the treatment plan. Similarly, your loved one who has an eating disorder (cancer) needs immediate, applicable treatment (CBT).

Another option is to meet with your church's women's ministry. See if they can directly mentor your loved one or connect you with a woman in the church body. I make sure to let women in our church know that I am willing and able to meet with those struggling. I have had two lovely ladies come my way, and we had some great coffee dates!

SURRENDER IT TO GOD

Ultimately, you must recognize that God is sovereign and has a plan even if your loved one has an eating disorder. You cannot fix it; only God can heal her. Of course, be proactive by setting a genuine and godly example for her. Listen to her and help provide her with the resources and encouragement she needs. Tell her that you love her and show her that you love her. Better yet, tell her that God loves her. And just as any loved one should do, pray for her. We do not know how or why God works through prayer, but he does. You may be the only one in her life aware of her struggle; pray for her recovery, but also pray for help in surrendering the burden you bear to God.

REFLECTION:

1. Question: What takeaways did you learn by reading through each coffee date? Do you have some recovery that needs to take place?

2. Action: Find a counselor or mentor for your loved one. Make a list and start reaching out.

3. Action: Pray for your loved one.

Bibliography

Borenstein, Jeffrey. "Self-love and What It Means." *Brain and Behavior Research Foundation*, February 12, 2020. https://www.bbrfoundation.org/blog/self-love-and-what-it-means.

"How Can I Have a Closer Relationship with God?" *Got Questions Ministries*, accessed December 5, 2021. https://www.gotquestions.org/closer-relationship-with-God.html.

Piper, John. "What Is Sin? The Essence and Root of All Sinning." *Desiring God*, February 2, 2015. https://www.desiringgod.org/messages/what-is-sin-the-essence-and-root-of-all-sinning.

Wilkin, Jen. "Should I Make My Child Apologize?" *The Gospel Coalition*, July 21, 2013. https://www.thegospelcoalition.org/article/should-i-make-my-child-apologize/.

Made in the USA
Las Vegas, NV
03 October 2023

78513435R00049